4/50



# BY MYSELF BUT NOT ALONE

## A PRAYER JOURNAL FOR DIVORCED MOMS

*Barbara Owen*

Judson Press ® Valley Forge, PA

By Myself, But Not Alone: A Prayer Journal for Divorced Moms


Judson Press, Valley Forge, PA 19482-0851



---

Library of Congress Cataloging-in-Publication Data
Owen, Barbara, 1935-
By myself but not alone : a prayer journal for divorced moms / Barbara Owen.
p. cm.
ISBN 0-8170-1201-X
1. Divorced mothers—Prayer-books and devotions—English.
2. Spiritual journals—Authorship. 3. Spiritual life—Christianity.
I. Title.
BV4596.D58094 1994
248.8'433—dc2093-42901 93-42901

---

Printed in the U.S.A.

# Contents

# Introduction

*Trust in the LORD with all your heart, and do not rely on your own insight. In all your ways acknowledge him, and he will make straight your paths. Proverbs 3:5-6*

Separation and divorce are difficult times in our lives, when our ability to trust may be shaky, yet we still reach out in hope, seeking guidance and strength from the Lord. The conversational prayers in this book came from talks with many mothers going through separation and divorce. Their children were infants, preschoolers, grade-schoolers, and a few young teens. The prayers are meant to put into words some of those thoughts and emotions that may be in your mind and heart. Some prayers may fit your situation; others may not, but will perhaps still bring a word of comfort.

Taken as a whole, each prayer and Scripture passage are meant for comfort, strength, insight, and nurture. The journal pages opposite each prayer are for your own prayer thoughts as they are prompted by the readings.

May Christ our Lord bless your devotional time and be your constant companion.

*"The joy that the LORD gives you will make you strong."*
*Nehemiah 8:10 (GNB)*

# Advent

*"'Prepare the way of the Lord, make his paths straight.'"*
*Mark 1:3*

O Lord, here I am getting out the Advent calendar. And the kids want me to make an Advent wreath "like you always do, Mom." I can't get in the mood this year, Lord. It's like I'm in a fog: one day is the same as another, one month the same as the one before. I'm kind of numb—when I'm not angry or worried.

How do I prepare your way this year, Lord? Will you do it for us? Make your paths straight in us, Lord, especially in me, that we can see you. The children cling to the traditions. I'm sorry not to feel more excitement. I always believed Advent was such a wonderful, spiritual time in the midst of the world's buying frenzy. Now I'm so rushed I didn't even pick up an Advent devotional booklet at church.

"Prepare the way of the Lord." Okay, what can we do to prepare your way now? What can we do amidst the rush of it all? You *are* willing and ready to do the preparing, aren't you, Lord? In the presence of all my confusion and emotional turmoil and busyness, you are here, right now, while I'm taping the torn doors on this Advent calendar. There's an Advent craft time at church next Sunday afternoon. The kids would like that. Okay, we'll go. Thanks, Lord, for opening my eyes and showing the way. We will celebrate Advent and prepare for Christmas. We need it.

*You prepare a table before me in the presence of my enemies.*
*Psalm 23:5*

# AIDS

*Surely he has borne our infirmities and carried our diseases;. . . But he was wounded for our transgressions, crushed for our iniquities; upon him was the punishment that made us whole.* Isaiah 53:4-5

O Lord, this disease confronts us like a brick wall. I think of marrying again. But how is a person safe from this infectious disease? I think I know myself, my self-control, my ability to be direct. But I know the pressure of human emotion. Even if I can stay celibate, will he have been? What can one expect in this odd time?

Isaiah wrote so long ago. Was even AIDS included in the diseases you carried for us? All transgressions and iniquities, infirmities and disease—you carried them all to the cross. I can believe that in my mind. But be with me in my heart, Jesus, to help me make right decisions about life now.

I know you care more than any human can. You didn't chastise the sick people of the day, saying, "How did you get this disease?" You healed and forgave sins and made whole. You loved and you gave instruction and power. Do that for me, Lord Christ.

*Bless the* LORD*, O my soul, and do not forget all his benefits—who forgives all your iniquity, who heals all your diseases, who redeems your life from the Pit, who crowns you with steadfast love and mercy.* Psalm 103:2-4

# Alone

*At my first defense no one came to my support, but all deserted me. May it not be counted against them! But the Lord stood by me and gave me strength.* 2 Timothy 4:16-17

There are times when I feel terribly alone, even with the children or other people around me. It's like divorce has never happened to anybody else before. But it has! What a large percentage of marriages end in divorce. Does every divorced person feel this alone, this different from other people, like no one really understands?

In the mall I see people, young and old, holding hands, laughing together. In restaurants couples are at every table. In the park birds are nesting. And I'm alone.

Do the children feel alone, too, Lord? Am I missing something? I'm afraid for them sometimes. Are they covering up their feelings? Your constant presence and reassurance are important to me. How can I help them to know you are with them, too?

*Seek the LORD and his strength; seek his presence continually. Remember the wonderful works he has done.*
*Psalm 105:4-5*

# Back Talk

*A gentle answer quiets anger, but a harsh one stirs it up. . . . Kind words bring life, but cruel words crush your spirit. . . . Hot tempers cause arguments, but patience brings peace.* Proverbs 15:1,4,18 (GNB)

I get so angry, Lord, when the children talk back to me. Where do they learn such nasty talk? And those words can hurt. How well I know that. Do children of divorce talk back more than other kids, or am I paranoid at times? But how words can hurt!

I guess you know that, Lord. Some people talked back to you when you were here. We still do when things aren't going well, even if the back talk is really only in our thoughts. I do it, too. Forgive me, Lord. But sometimes when I feel like yelling at you, I read or hear your Word and it calms my spirit. And often you have just the right word for me.

Help me to do that for the children, Lord. Help me to bear with the back talk that comes from their anger at a situation, or The Situation. Help me to forgive and find a right word to say at the right time.

Lord, you calm my troubled heart. Even now as I think about what my son said yesterday, I begin to understand. He was angry about what happened at school more than at me. His words were cruel, but you gave me strength. Your words give life. Give me the patience that brings peace, Lord. Let my words be kind to him, even when Imust say no to a request. Let me be an example of kindnessin speech that the children may learn it, too.

*What a joy it is to find just the right word for the right occasion!* Proverbs 15:23 (GNB)

# Birds

*And God said, "Let the waters bring forth swarms of living creatures, and let birds fly above the earth across the dome of the sky." So God created the great sea monsters and . . . every winged bird of every kind. And God saw that it was good.*
*Genesis 1:20-21*

"Birdies! See 'em!" my son said this morning from his booster chair at the table. He pointed out the window, so excited. Thank you, Lord, for letting me see "birdies" again with new eyes. And so many kinds of birds. The goldfinches are turning bright yellow, the cardinals are like red ornaments on the evergreen trees, the brown sparrows jump backward on the ground, scratching for seeds.

Thank you, Lord, for the birds and for this child who has helped me to stop and have a look. With all the technology around today, it's become easy to take your creation for granted. But it is all amazing and beautiful. And it is comforting, Lord, to remember that you who made all things are the One who cares for me, guides my life, renews me and gives strength, even at times like these—especially at times like these.

If you can make something as intricate and delicate as a hummingbird and as bold and powerful as an eagle, surely you can and will care for me. Thanks for spots of joy along the way, the joy that came today watching the birdies. See 'em!

*My help comes from the LORD, who made heaven and earth. Psalm 121:2*

# Child Care

*"The LORD watch between you and me, when we are absent one from the other." Genesis 31:49*

It was all set, Lord. A Christian home, the woman accepted only a few children, my daughter liked it there—I really felt you were watching between the child and me while we were apart. And between Ms. Nancy and me. But now she has developed an illness and can take children only part-time. You know I need all day, five days a week.

Lord, this child care business tears at my insides. Just when I think it's finally settled, it falls apart. Guide me in finding new care. Help me not to be so angry because of being divorced and having it all fall on me to do. My shoulders are small, Lord, and the burden of care is huge.

Help me to have some peace so I can think straight. Guide my thinking, so that a new situation can be worked out. It's so easy to concentrate only on the difficult parts of life. Nudge me to consider the positive things going on for us. My daughter's potty trained, at last. That's a plus! And maybe that will make it easier to find child care.

Lord, help me to find a situation that will be a blessing to my daughter and a reinforcement for me in helping her to grow. You love her even more than I do. It's hard to remember that, but I know it's true. Out of your love for her, guide me in this child care matter, dear Lord.

*[Jesus] took [the children] up in his arms, laid his hands on them, and blessed them. Mark 10:16*

# Child Support

*Religion that is pure and undefiled before God, the Father, is this: to care for orphans and widows in their distress, and to keep oneself unstained by the world. James 1:27*

I suppose divorced moms and their children are sort of like the orphans and widows of Bible times. I like to think so, Lord, when I read how concerned you were for their welfare.

It is incredibly tough, Lord. I shake when I open the mailbox at this time each month—child support time. Usually the check is there. I'm lucky. Denise hasn't received a check in six months. Laurel never knows what amount will be on hers. Lord, be with these moms, too. We need some peace about this issue. Just seeing his handwriting on the check makes my stomach knot up and my teeth clench. Involuntary stress signs, someone said.

Lord, when I think of how many women struggle with child support payments, it's overwhelming. Ease the tension, Lord. Help me to remember that because you care, you will not forsake us. Help me to set priorities on necessities for living.

*When I thought, "My foot is slipping," your steadfast love, O LORD, held me up. When the cares of my heart are many, your consolations cheer my soul. Psalm 94:18-19*

# Christmas

*And she gave birth to her firstborn son and wrapped him in bands of cloths, and laid him in a manger, because there was no place for them in the inn. Luke 2:7*

Surely Mary felt lonely when she gave birth to Jesus, maybe as strange and out of step with life as I feel this Christmas. Everything is different. I'd always thought of the manger scene as sweet and joyful, Lord. But here was Mary in this strange and crowded city instead of back home where her family would be near, where a midwife would come, probably someone she knew. In her heart she knew something wonderful was happening. But being a first-time mother had to be scary—and then the angels and shepherds—the confusion. I feel confusion this Christmas, Lord.

Yet Mary must have felt some sort of peace, too, that kind that comes from you, Lord—that peace that is beyond our understanding. It happens for me once in a while. In the middle of some terrible situation, I'll think, How can I feel so peaceful? That's when I know it's from you.

I need that peace this Christmas, Jesus, as I try to help the children celebrate. They'll be with their father part of the time, though. Help me to remember that Christmas isn't just a family time but a day to reflect on your coming to be our savior, our peace, our reconciliation, our brother. As I read the Christmas story anew, let me, like Mary, treasure the words and ponder them in my heart.

*When [the shepherds] saw this, they made known what had been told them about this child; . . . Mary treasured all these words and pondered them in her heart. Luke 2:17,19*

# Crying—Mine

*I am weary with my crying; my throat is parched. My eyes grow dim with waiting for my God.* *Psalm 69:3*

Why am I crying so often when we talk, God? No one else knows how much I cry. Some think I'm strong. "She's doing so well," I heard one tell another. If they only knew the turmoil inside.

I'm sick and tired of crying, Lord. I guess it's supposed to let out harmful stuff from inside, but I'm tired of it. Crying in church when I least expect it. Crying on the way to work. Crying after the children are in bed. Crying when I hear certain music. Oh, Lord, I'm weary of it, so weary of the sadness, the crying.

I'm glad you have psalm verses about crying in the Bible, Lord. People cried with you in Bible times. Even Jesus cried. Are you crying with me now, Jesus? I guess you are because you share our sorrows. Then if you cry with me, you will also give me peace and get me through these days. Surely we can look ahead to happier times. I'll wait.

*Give ear, O LORD, to my prayer; listen to my cry of supplication. In the day of my trouble I call on you, for you will answer me.* *Psalm 86:6-7*

# Crying—Theirs

*Blessed be the God and Father of our Lord Jesus Christ, the Father of mercies and the God of all consolation, who consoles us in all our affliction, so that we may be able to console those who are in any affliction with the consolation with which we ourselves are consoled by God.*
*2 Corinthians 1:3-4*

They cry at the least expected times, Lord, or at the least convenient times. Sometimes it unnerves me and I yell at them. I'm sorry. Tonight I put the youngest to bed early. Was that fair? I hate to see him crying so much lately. Only Melanie doesn't cry, but I think she's crying inside and won't let it out.

I want them not to be affected, to get on with their lives. I guess that's not realistic at all. They *are* affected by the divorce; they don't know what kind of life to get on with. O Lord, make me strong enough to be a patient parent, to hear their cries and give comfort, just as you do for me. You care for me through friends and the counselor, through your Word and worship. How do I bring caring comfort to the children?

Help me to let them talk about what they're thinking, even if it hurts me. Help me to hold them when they cry and don't know why. Help me to acknowledge their sadness and together look for ways to love one another.

*As an eagle stirs up its nest, and hovers over its young; as it spreads its wings, takes them up, and bears them aloft on its pinions, the LORD alone guided him.*
*Deuteronomy 32:11-12*

# Custody

*I pray that the God of our Lord Jesus Christ . . . may give you a spirit of wisdom and revelation as you come to know him, so that, with the eyes of your heart enlightened, you may know what is the hope to which he has called you.*
*Ephesians 1:17-18*

Custody, visitation rights—words I never thought would apply to my family, Lord. It's hard to work these arrangements out, even though they're down on paper. It's his weekend to take the children, but he can't because of business out of town. He wants them next weekend instead, but that's when my sister's coming.

This kind of thing happens all the time, Lord. The kids are ping-ponging back and forth between households. Sometimes it's regular, sometimes it's not.

Lord, forgive me for getting so wrapped up in my own emotions about this. Be with the children. Help them to have a "normal" life, whatever that is anymore. Let them feel loved by both parents. Help me to hear what they want to do in these situations. Give me strength to be firm when I need to be, relaxed about arrangements when that is best for the children. Give me that wisdom that can come only from you, Lord.

*But the wisdom from above is first pure, then peaceable, gentle, willing to yield, full of mercy and good fruits, without a trace of partiality or hypocrisy. And a harvest of righteousness is sown in peace for those who make peace.*
*James 3:17-18*

# Dating

*I am like an owl of the wilderness, like a little owl of the waste places. I lie awake; I am like a lonely bird on the housetop.*
*Psalm 102:6-7*

Yes, Lord, I'm lonely. I have been lonely for a long time, I realize now. When Tim from work asked me to lunch it was so pleasant. And now we're going to a concert. A part of me feels lifted up, but part of me is afraid. Dating—it's confusing. Is it too soon? But I'm lonely.

When Dad started dating three months after Mom died I was shocked and hurt. I wasn't very nice to him. Forgive me, Lord. Now I see he was lonely, too.

Help me to understand the children's confusion. What are they thinking about Tim? Are they hiding, covering up what they really feel?

Lord, help me to be sensible, to care for my own needs while understanding the children's needs. Let me not impose my own needs on them.

You suffered terrible loneliness, Jesus. You understand. Give me peace and teach me to be sensible. Show me many ways to cope with this loneliness.

*Now may the Lord of peace himself give you peace at all times in all ways. The Lord be with all of you.*
*2 Thessalonians 3:16*

# Divorced

*They [Paul and Barnabas] had such a sharp disagreement that they parted company. Barnabas took Mark and sailed for Cyprus, but Paul chose Silas and left. Acts 15:39-40 (NIV)*

Divorced, separated—I hate those words, Lord. I hate having to say "I'm divorced" when asked about my marital status. When filling out a form, I hate marking the little block that says "divorced" rather than "married" or "single." Even though probably half the people who check "married" now will sometime have to check "divorced," I feel as if I'm the only one.

The other day I came across the passage in the Bible about Paul and Barnabas and their big fight and separation. It wasn't a marriage splitting up, but they were close friends and Christian workers. Surely all their Christian friends prayed for them about this disagreement. Surely other Christians counseled the two. But with all the prayers and trust in you, the sad but only solution seems to have been for the two to part. Did they each seek forgiveness, Lord? Was one or the other to blame? Who knows now, but we can read the Bible and know their work went on. Your work went on through these two people who disagreed so much they had to separate.

Lord, help me to go on. Don't let me get stuck thinking too much about what has happened. Help me to accept your love and forgiveness and to move ahead with the strength you give.

*With everlasting love I will have compassion on you, says the LORD, your Redeemer. Isaiah 54:8*

# Easter

*I write these things to you who believe in the name of the Son of God, so that you may know that you have eternal life.*
*1 John 5:13*

*"Go quickly and tell his disciples, 'He has been raised from the dead, and indeed he is going ahead of you to Galilee; there you will see him.' This is my message for you."*
*Matthew 28:7*

"Going ahead of you to Galilee"? How did the angel know the disciples would go to Galilee? That's back home, where they used to fish. It's as if the angel was telling these mixed-up people, "Jesus is going to see you at home. In fact, he'll probably get there before you do."

This is sort of what the pastor was saying in the Easter message today, Lord, that you're right here with us in our everyday life. I suppose that's what makes our ordinary life the "abundant life" even when it seems otherwise. Help this to sink in for me, Lord. It's easier to know eternal life is coming. Today's life as a divorced mom seems abundant only in hurry and worry and pressure.

Be with us in our Easter celebration here at home, Lord. Let every Easter egg the children find remind us of your resurrection and your presence with us this very day.

*"I came that they may have life, and have it abundantly."*
*John 10:10*

# Emotions

*Deliver me from my enemies, O my God; protect me from those who rise up against me.* *Psalm 59:1*

"Your emotions are raw," my counselor told me. She's right. They feel like enemies, Lord, and they do rise up against me. Anger gushes up from deep inside when something he said long ago is triggered in my memory. I feel ambushed by these memories and the anger that wells up. That's not me, Lord. I am shocked at myself, but I have to admit it's there in order to let it out. Take it away, Lord, the anger and the fear, too.

Yesterday I thought I saw him for a moment. It was someone else in the bank line, but the old knot had come to my stomach and the pain in the back. It just happens, Lord, these unannounced emotions.

I pray for peacefulness, Lord, a bit of joy now and then. Be with me on this roller coaster ride of emotions. I know the end will come; the smoother track does lie ahead. You are with me now and you will be with me then, too.

The hardest is dealing with the baby when anger or fear attacks. She doesn't understand my tears. Maybe I better keep seeing the counselor. Maybe that's one of the ways you are delivering me from the enemies. Thank you, Lord.

*"Peace I leave with you; my peace I give to you. I do not give to you as the world gives. Do not let your hearts be troubled, and do not let them be afraid."* *John 14:27*

# Everything I Have to Do

*No one serving in the army gets entangled in everyday affairs;
the soldier's aim is to please the enlisting officer.*
*2 Timothy 2:4*

This Bible verse jumped out at me this morning, Lord. I've been reading a little in some of these short books in the Bible, and I must admit my mind was more on all I have to do today and this week than on the reading. I kept pulling my attention back to the words. And then this verse popped out.

Is Paul telling Timothy to watch his priorities? Are you telling me that? It's so tough to set priorities because everything needs to be done. And yet, there's only one parent here now. I can't do it all. What can I leave out and be fair to the kids? Fair to me? Fair to my employer? Fair to friends and family? Fair to you, Lord?

Maybe I can at least see what must be done today and what can be put off. Help me with that, Lord. My friend who goes to AA keeps saying she tries to live "one day at a time." Show me the needs of just this day, Lord.

The soldier isn't the officer, who has to think of the battle ahead. The soldier thinks of just that day's business. And what was it you said? "Today's trouble is enough for today." Help me to plan for today and trust you with the other days. Save me from being frantic, Lord.

*I will satisfy the weary, and all who are faint I will replenish.*
*Jeremiah 31:25*

# Everything's Going Wrong

*Though the fig tree does not blossom, and no fruit is on the vines; though the produce of the olive fails and the fields yield no food; though the flock is cut off from the fold and there is no herd in the stalls, yet I will rejoice in the LORD; I will exult in the God of my salvation. GOD, the Lord, is my strength.*
*Habakkuk 3:17-19*

I might have guessed Timmy would flush a toy and make the toilet run over. I might have figured Sarah would give up being potty trained, with all the tension of these times. I might have known I'd have the first flat tire of my life. But Lord, the bird in the house this morning was just too much. A starling yet, zooming around like the *Concorde*!

At least the neighbor was home to help, and we managed to get the bird out the back door. But now there are sooty marks to clean up, since it must have come down the chimney. That means calling someone to put a barrier in there. It never ends, Lord.

Then I read the passage from Habakkuk tonight. He paints a dreadful picture. Yet he still says he can rejoice in you, Lord! Well, maybe. Were you in the neighbor who helped with the bird? Was it you who nudged me to sign up for emergency road service before the flat tire happened? And maybe you're showing me that Sarah needs extra attention now. I don't know about the toy in the toilet, Lord! I get exhausted remembering all this. Yet I feel a strength, too, because I *was* able to cope. We *are* doing okay.

*But you do see [Lord]! Indeed you note trouble and grief, that you may take it into your hands. Psalm 10:14*

# Exercise

*"'You shall love the Lord your God with all your heart, and with all your soul, and with all your mind, and with all your strength.'" Mark 12:30*

Lord, give me energy to get through this exercise video tonight. Here I am, bouncing with the beat and I can think of about a million things I'd rather be doing. Keep me at it, Lord. I know I need it for myself and for the kids.

The pastor explained that verse about heart (emotions), soul (personality or entire being), mind (mental capacity), and strength (body). Broken down like that, I can see that the condition of my body does affect my emotions and my thoughts—well, my entire being.

Remind me of how much better I feel after one of these sessions, Lord. Keep nudging me to exercise. I'd like to find a class, but then there's babysitting to pay for. Cheryl gets up early in the morning to exercise before her kids are up. Forget that! Tanya can go out running while her husband gets breakfast. Nice. And here I am after the kids are in bed and I'm almost there myself.

Maybe this is okay for now. It doesn't have to be forever. Maybe down the road a bit I'll be able to do something more fun for exercise. Help me keep it all in balance, Lord—the heart, soul, mind, and strength stuff—so I can be a whole person for the children, for you, for me.

*I will greatly rejoice in the LORD,*
*my whole being shall exult in my God;*
*for he has clothed me with the garments of salvation,*
*he has covered me with the robe of righteousness.*
*Isaiah 61:10*

# Faith

*Simon Peter answered him, "Lord, to whom can we go? You have the words of eternal life. We have come to believe and know that you are the Holy One of God." John 6:68-69*

O Lord, some days my faith is so shaky. I don't even know if I have faith or not. But you are the one I turn to in my deepest need. Even when I don't know if I believe or not, I talk to you. I pick up the Bible and read. Sometimes the words speak to me and I am assured. Sometimes the words don't say much at all. But I'm always glad to have read them.

Faith is an odd kind of trust, a trust without seeing, a trust that's hard to explain. It seems to go back and forth between people. At church on some Sundays it's like I catch faith from others. And I know on my "up" days I'm able to give some faith away.

Did you make it work that way, Lord, so your people would need each other? Thank you for my congregation where faith is nurtured. Guide my friend Anne whose congregation doesn't seem to know what to do with divorced people. Thank you for the times with the children when faith is strong and growing and shared. Hold us during those foggy times when faith seems like mist. We will wait because faith is not something we do but something you do in us.

*For in hope we were saved. Now hope that is seen is not hope. For who hopes for what is seen? But if we hope for what we do not see, we wait for it with patience. Romans 8:24-25*

# Friends

*David went out to meet them and said to them, "If you have come to me in friendship, to help me, then my heart will be knit to you; but if you have come to betray me to my adversaries, though my hands have done no wrong, then may the God of our ancestors see and give judgment."*
*1 Chronicles 12:17*

Some friends have been really special, Lord, knowing what to say and what not to say. Others aren't really friends anymore. Divorce seems to bring out caring or judgment in people.

I was feeling guilty about being angry at Pat until I read this verse. I feel so down after being with her. But now I think it's okay to avoid her, to seek companionship with friends who build up instead of tear down.

When I've talked with a caring friend I'm better with the children, too. When friends hear my sorrow or complaints, I don't dump my emotions on the children. Thank you for the network of friends who are my safety net. They are like your hands holding me up. They are like your ears listening. And some are like your mouth giving words of hope and comfort.

Some friends are family, too—a double blessing. But other family members have not been friends during this time. I can overlook that, since I, too, have been judgmental in the past. Now I'm sorry. Bless them all, Lord; I thank you especially for the caring friends and family.

*A friend loves at all times, and kinsfolk are born to share adversity. Proverbs 17:17*

# Gardening

*Jesus said to her, "Woman, why are you weeping? Whom are you looking for?" Supposing him to be the gardener, she said to him, "Sir, if you have carried him away, tell me. . . ." Jesus said to her, "Mary!"  John 20:15-16*

Lord, sometimes I think you're saying my name when I'm in the garden, too. I don't know what the garden was like where your tomb was. But if Mary Magdalene expected to find the gardener when she saw the resurrected you, it must have been a well-tended place. What an unexpected joy for her to find the "gardener" was *you.*

My few plants get neglected these days, with all I have to do. But when I see them withering and remember to water them, they perk up. Even a few minutes watering or digging in the dirt or repotting plants perks me up, too. Maybe people are right when they say that getting close to nature makes them feel closer to God.

Thanks for meeting me in my gardening, Jesus. I feel loved.

*The LORD will guide you continually, and satisfy your needs in parched places, and make your bones strong; and you shall be like a watered garden, like a spring of water, whose waters never fail.  Isaiah 58:11*

# God Talk

*Recite [these commandments] to your children and talk about them when you are at home and when you are away, when you lie down and when you rise. Deuteronomy 6:7*

"God bless you," she said when I turned in for the night. Your name, Lord, was such a blessing in that simple phrase, a phrase some people would call trite. The children were with their father for the weekend and I was with this dear friend and her family. We talked of many things, but what I remember most were her words of faith and trust and blessing in that simple phrase when I went to the guest room for the night. "God bless you," she said. Your name, coming like that of a most special friend, with peace and joy, made my heart glad, for I knew then that you, Lord, were there in that household and with me.

Is this the kind of mentioning of your name and will that you meant in your Word? Often we are too rushed for long talks about you, but a word of blessing can remind the children and me that we are your children. Help us always to remember table prayers. Help me to remember to talk about Sunday school or church when we're on the way home or later in the day. Let me not be so rushed with the strain of divorced life that I forget little ways to talk with the children about your life.

*We will tell to the coming generation the glorious deeds of the LORD. Psalm 78:4*

# Guilt/Shame

*He does not deal with us according to our sins, nor repay us according to our iniquities. For as the heavens are high above the earth, so great is his steadfast love toward those who fear him; as far as the east is from the west, so far he removes our transgressions from us. Psalm 103:10-12*

Lord, I know you know when I've been wrong. Not just things I might have done differently in the marriage. I'm thinking of the everyday things in dealing with the children. I get so mad at myself when I yell at them because I'm tired. I feel guilty leaving them with a sitter at night when they've been at day care all day. But sometimes I have to. There's no other way. I end up feeling guilty about things I shouldn't feel guilty about as well as things I should. Help me, Lord, to know your healing forgiveness again today. Make me new again.

And keep away the arrows of shame hurled at divorced moms by society. I know things aren't as bad as they were years ago. But there are still the looks, the innuendos in conversations, things said and not said that try to heap shame on divorced mothers.

Help me to know every day that I am your forgiven child, that you love me and my children, that you walk with us in friendship every single day.

*But you, O LORD, are a shield around me, my glory, and the one who lifts up my head. Psalm 3:3*

# He Left

*The LORD protects the simple; when I was brought low, he saved me. Psalm 116:6*

You can't be brought much lower than to have your husband leave you, Lord. The father of your children leaves you for some other woman. Now his "fling" is over, but he's still finding out who he is, out there somewhere.

I know what some people say, Lord. There must have been something missing in the marriage for him or he wouldn't have left. And I say it to myself. What could I have done differently? We've been over this a million times, Lord, but here I am asking you, asking myself, what?

I do feel very simple, Lord, like a child myself sometimes, here with my children. My parents have been understanding, but I don't want to lean on them too much. Help me to lean on you, Lord. I'm coming to you like a little child, just as you said we should. Help me to move ahead in life, wherever, whatever that means.

This psalmist says you saved him when he was brought low. I sure am low, Lord. Help me for the sake of the children, for my sake, even for your sake because I am your child.

*The LORD is near to the brokenhearted, and saves the crushed in spirit. Psalm 34:18*

# I Left

*The LORD will keep your going out and your coming in from this time on and forevermore. Psalm 121:8*

I go over it again and again, Lord. It must have been the right decision—the marriage couldn't go on. The counseling had gone nowhere. But here I am having doubts again. Yesterday I was fine, moving ahead with resolve. Now I am crying on the way to work again, just like I left Jamie crying at day care.

Have I cheated my child out of a "normal" two-parent life? Were kids better off when parents "stayed together for the children," even when one or the other's mental and emotional health was being damaged? There are too many decisions, Lord. It's so tough. I have to be so tough. Why do I feel so unsure today?

I thought I'd feel better when the separation came. At first it was such a relief. Now I'm confused. I talk to Carolyn, whose situation is completely different. Her husband left her with a three-month-old baby and a child in grade school. No wonder she's frantic and depressed. But sometimes I feel like that, too. When will it be better?

I guess I'm on the roller coaster again, and now I'm at the bottom. Surely it will be going up again. Lord, if you keep my going out and coming in, if you're with me always—and I really believe you are or I wouldn't be talking to you here in the car—then help me to wait out this attack. Give me a little peace, just for today.

*You are indeed my rock and my fortress; for your name's sake lead me and guide me. Psalm 31:3*

# Jealousy

*Let us live honorably as in the day, . . . not in quarreling and jealousy.* *Romans 13:13*

Jealousy is like poison ivy, Lord. I didn't think I could get it, but lately I've been itching all over with it. I find myself being jealous of married friends, of anyone who seems to have enough money to spend on extras, of the new woman at work who is so self-confident, whose hair always looks perfect.

I don't want to be like this, Lord. It upsets me when my son expresses jealous feelings about some friend's new Nintendo game or tennis shoes. Often he's jealous over material things, and I guess I am, too. Our jealousy is a kind of coveting, wanting something another has—or something just like it.

Lord, teach me contentment, and show me how to teach contentment with what we have to my son. I remember something Grampa said about people he visited in a third-world country. I was looking at his pictures of a smiling family outside a one-room house. "They don't have things," Grampa said. "They have each other." Lord, give us contentment, so that we won't be jealous or covetous of anything.

*I have learned to be satisfied with what I have. I know what it is to be in need and what it is to have more than enough. I have learned this secret, so that anywhere, at any time, I am content, . . . whether I have too much or too little. I have the strength to face all conditions by the power that Christ gives me.*
*Philippians 4:11-13 (GNB)*

# Journal

*"Write, therefore, what you have seen, what is now and what will take place later." Revelation 1:19 (NIV)*

O Lord, you commanded many of your people to write what they understood about you. Their words would help others, but I imagine the words were helpful to those writing, too. Sometimes the very act of writing is tonic for me as well; other times I'm afraid of my thoughts and won't write them down on paper. Help me to write, Lord. It would help me to get out those angry and fearful thoughts.

Surely you understand. How many psalms tell about trouble and misery and anger. I feel angry and afraid at times, Lord. But after I've listed my woes, I begin to remember your past goodness to me. I begin to hope again.

I count on your understanding, God. I can tell you things I can tell no one else. Thank you for loving me so much that I'm not afraid you'll be shocked by my angry feelings. You hear the words I put on paper. You lead on to a new place where I can write something else, maybe a letter to cheer a friend, or a note to someone who is shut-in. What a miracle that you can do that, like bringing water out of a rock. I thank and praise you, O God.

*[The Lord said to Moses,] "Strike the rock, and water will come out of it, so that the people may drink."*
*Exodus 17:6*

# Kindness

*Be kind to one another, tenderhearted, forgiving one another, as God in Christ has forgiven you. Ephesians 4:32*

Lord, kindness takes time and gentleness. It's hard to feel kind or to be kind when you feel rushed, stressed, pushed. Children learn kindness by example, I think, but there's not much kindness around in the world. And by the time I get home from work and they're home from school, all our kindness seems used up. That's not right. Help us, Lord.

I know how one word or act of kindness can bring peace. Kindness can be contagious. Help me to speak and act kindly at home. Help me to encourage the children to be kind to each other and to me.

The other evening my son put my favorite music tape on the player, forgoing his own loud rock band. That little kindness made our whole evening better.

Help us to remember your continuing kindness to us and thus to be kind to one another.

*When the goodness and loving kindness of God our Savior appeared, he saved us, not because of any works of righteousness that we had done, but according to his mercy. Titus 3:4-5*

# Laughter

*There the ships go to and fro, and the leviathan, which you formed to frolic there.* Psalm 104:26 (NIV)

*Glory in his holy name; let the hearts of those who seek the* LORD *rejoice.* Psalm 105:3

Lord, you made us, you know us. You made us to laugh. Last night the kids and I laughed until we cried over that silly video. Thank you. Thank you for the gift of laughter that can bring peace and lightness and closeness to those who laugh together. Now that I think about it, I can see that laughter got lost in the marriage a long time ago. I've missed laughing.

Some people think you're all seriousness, Lord. But you wouldn't call serious people to rejoice. Rejoicing means smiles, joyfulness, singing. Even your creation shows your humor. Just look at the frolicking sea creatures! And giraffes—really!

Help us to see this joy and humor in creation, Lord, as well as the beauty. Help me to rest so securely in you that I can laugh. It's easy to get so caught up in my responsibilities that I can't relax enough to laugh.

Lord, for my sake, for the children's sake, give me laughter. It is a precious gift, not a frivolous extra.

*Let the rivers clap their hands, let the mountains sing together for joy; let them sing before the* LORD. Psalm 98:8-9a (NIV)

# Lent

*Return to the LORD, your God, for he is gracious and merciful, slow to anger, and abounding in steadfast love.*
*Joel 2:13*

Before now, Lent has seemed like an old-fashioned tradition that some Christians talked about more than others. But, Lord, it is very real for me this year. Lent is a time of waiting and pondering, of watching for spring to arrive and of preparing to celebrate Easter. But part of this Lent for me is some sort of longing I feel to be closer to you, Lord.

The bulletin from church lists Bible readings for each day of the week. I've been trying to do the readings, and they help. I want to feel your love all around me, like a child sitting on a parent's lap. At those times when I feel your love, I seem to be nicer to the children.

But other times I feel at loose ends. I'm angry at myself, and I don't feel lovable at all. Are those times meant to call us back to you, Lord, to prayer, to reading your Word? If that's so, then here I am. Keep me near to you this Lent, Lord. Open my heart so that your love can come in.

*I wait for the LORD, my soul waits, and in his word I hope; . . . For with the LORD there is steadfast love, and . . . great power to redeem.* *Psalm 130:5,7*

# Living Water

*Jesus answered her, "If you knew the gift of God, and who it is that is saying to you, 'Give me a drink,' you would have asked him, and he would have given you living water."*
*John 4:10*

You give something very special, Jesus—living water. Not stagnant or foul water, but water that gives life. I've been thinking about the woman at the well to whom you spoke words about living water. Your presence with her, your words, turned her life around—gave her a new life, it seems. And her words to others were also like living water to them. They came to know you and believe in you, too.

Thank you for people who have been living water in my life, renewing my spirit. Thanks for unexpected joys that are living water for me and the children. Today the art exhibit in the lobby of the bank lifted me out of myself. Was that living water? The rainbow my little Ashley saw this week for the first time—was that living water? The new Bible class at church Sunday morning—surely that's living water.

*"If you knew. . .you would have asked."* I have been asking, Lord, haven't I? And you have been giving, haven't you? Open my eyes, my ears, my heart to recognize the living water you give in so many ways.

*"Let anyone who is thirsty come to me, and let the one who believes in me drink. As the scripture has said, 'Out of the believer's heart shall flow rivers of living water.'"*
*John 7:37-38*

# Mealtime (with a toddler)

*Better to eat vegetables with people you love than to eat the finest meat where there is hate. Proverbs 15:17 (GNB)*

O Lord, I'm so tired of coaxing this little person I love to eat his vegetables. Often my love hides inside. I get exasperated and my tone of voice becomes harsh. And then he'll say something to make me laugh, and I'm ashamed of my impatience.

But it never ends, Lord. He'll hardly wait for the prayer, then stuff too much food in his mouth at once. Or he'll eat two bites and say "All done" and "Down, down" in that insistent toddler voice. It's so hard, Lord, handling a toddler alone. It's so hard not having any real conversation at mealtime. I save my own dessert until after he's in bed, then eat with the folks on television. What kind of life is this?

I know it won't always be so. He will grow and learn to talk and move past these difficult stages. We do have a friend or relative in now and then for a meal. Although the other adult can be unnerved by my toddler, it's such a relief to me to have an adult to talk with. Bless those people who come to our dinner table, Lord. They don't know how much they mean in my life. And bless those who invite us out. Is it you, Lord, reaching out to us through others? I think you do understand. Thanks for just hearing me out today.

*When he was at the table with them, he took bread, blessed and broke it, and gave it to them. Luke 24:30*

# Money

*If we have food and clothing, we will be content with these. But those who want to be rich fall into temptation and are trapped by many senseless and harmful desires that plunge people into ruin and destruction. 1 Timothy 6:8-9*

I wish I didn't get so upset about money, Lord. It's almost a sickness in our society. So many words are written or spoken every day about how to get it, keep it, spend it. The kids get caught up in this sickness, too. I ask one to do an extra chore and it's "How much do I get?" Or I find myself bribing them to be good, giving "bonuses" or extracting "fines" for behavior. Is that too much attention on money?

It's on my mind because our budget is so tight. What do we really need? How can we find free entertainment? The TV pictures of homeless families scare me. How do I manage the household money without constant worry? Help me to find methods. Help me to trust. I know one thing, constant worry about money doesn't help at all.

*Keep your lives free from the love of money, and be content with what you have; for he has said, "I will never leave you or forsake you." So we can say with confidence, "The Lord is my helper; I will not be afraid." Hebrews 13:5-6*

# My Birthday

*O LORD, you have searched me and known me. You know when I sit down and when I rise up; you discern my thoughts from far away. You . . . are acquainted with all my ways. . . . For it was you who formed my inward parts; you knit me together in my mother's womb.  Psalm 139:1-3,13*

I never thought I'd have a birthday like this, Lord. So empty. It wasn't a *bad* day—people at work took me out for lunch, and the kids remembered. It wasn't like some past birthdays that were filled with tension. But, I have questions this year. Who am I? I don't know anymore. Why do I feel so empty?

Birthdays are milestones when people look back and look ahead. But I don't want to look back. Looking ahead is hopeful some days, scary other days. What will life be like by my next birthday? Will the emptiness still be here? It's scary, Lord.

Will I be single forever now? Will I marry again? I dream of a happy marriage and family life. But I'm not about to settle for just anyone. How will I know? I have so many questions, Lord, on this birthday. Guide me, lead me, love me, Lord.

*The LORD will fulfill his purpose for me; your steadfast love, O LORD, endures forever. Do not forsake the work of your hands.  Psalm 138:8*

# New Year's Day

*Jesus Christ is the same yesterday and today and forever.*
*Hebrews 13:8*

A new year, Lord. The year lies ahead of us, with a crisp calendar of unspoiled pages, the anticipation of holidays, opportunities for new learning for the children. Let it be a year of hope, Lord.

I know there will be pain, but this year can the hope and peace start to outweigh the pain? Beginnings have always been times of hope for me. A fresh piece of paper, the start of a new class, a new project at home.

Lord, I look at the calendar and wonder what will fill its pages. This is really a time to step out in faith, isn't it? My life, the children, the world all change, but you are the same. You have always been loving, caring, redeeming, and strengthening your people. Because I can count on you to keep being this way, I *can* look ahead to the new year in hope.

*"Be strong and bold; have no fear or dread . . . because it is the* L*ORD your God who goes with you; he will not fail you or forsake you." Deuteronomy 31:6*

# Nighttime Thoughts

*I will both lie down and sleep in peace; for you alone, O LORD, make me lie down in safety. Psalm 4:8*

I want this psalm verse to be true for me, Lord, but the truth is I don't always sleep in peace. If I go to sleep, I wake in the middle of the night. The weird thoughts come—like when I was a kid and the night was full of monsters and creatures out to get me. Now the "what ifs" come.

What if I lose my job? What if I never marry again? What if I do marry and have stepchildren—will we get along? What if Jason wants to live with his dad when he gets older?

The "what ifs" come and I imagine myself living in these different situations. Why do I put myself through this torment, Lord? Am I trying to be prepared for what might come?

But I need sleep tonight. Help me to live my life now, just in the moment, knowing that you are here no matter what. Give me peaceful bedtime thoughts, Lord. I try to make bedtime pleasant and secure for Jason. Help me to do that for myself, Lord, knowing that you are here with me as I sleep. And if I wake in the night, you'll be here then, too. Turn my thoughts to you whenever I awake.

*The LORD is my shepherd, I shall not want. He makes me lie down in green pastures; he leads me beside still waters; he restores my soul. Psalm 23:1-3*

# The Other Parent (I)

*Thou dost keep him in perfect peace, whose mind is stayed on thee, because he trusts in thee. Trust in the LORD for ever, for the LORD GOD is an everlasting rock. Isaiah 26:3-4 (RSV)*

O God, when will it be easier? The children go to visit their other parent and I am torn apart. The free time is welcome, but my mind keeps seeing pictures of the kids with the "other."

Every time they go I tell myself I won't ask questions when they return, but I can't seem to help it. The kids mention one thing and I'm off, cross-examining them. What's going on in his life? I wonder. And all the time I'm thinking, Do the kids have fun there? Do they have as much fun with me?

Lord, why can't I just be glad they enjoy both of their parents? Why can't I be glad for them, like I am when they visit the grandparents? The pain is so great. Anguish—I never knew what it was before, and I hate it.

You knew emotional pain too, didn't you, Jesus? You suffered physical pain, but maybe the emotional pain was worse as you cried for your people. See my emotions; they are raw with hurting. Touch me with your healing. Help me not to hate, not to think with pain about the other. Give me new thoughts, Lord, new emotions, new peace.

*The peace of God, which surpasses all understanding, will guard your hearts and your minds in Christ Jesus.*
*Philippians 4:7*

# The Other Parent (II)

*"I will forgive their sins and will no longer remember their wrongs." Hebrews 8:12 (GNB)*

I read these words, Lord, and know it is possible for you to do what you've promised. You do forgive; you do forget. When I feel my life moving ahead, sometimes I think I am close to forgiving because you make it possible. I can't forget everything that's happened in the past because I don't want to make my own mistakes again. Any new relationship must be different.

Lord, I've told you about everything, all the anger, the hurt, the confusion. I've told the counselor most of it, too. I've told some of it to other people, but I try not to tell too much. It wouldn't be fair to the children or to their father. But sometimes it's hard not to tell, to try to justify myself. Help me, Lord. We still have to deal with each other about the children.

A few days ago I met a woman who was complaining bitterly about her ex-husband. Her pain sounded more recent than mine. I spoke sympathetically to her, asking how long it had been. Eighteen years, she said. Eighteen years! O Lord, I don't want to feel this way eighteen years from now. Lord, help me focus on positive thoughts and goals. Lord, bless both of us parents, so that this doesn't happen to us.

*The whole law is summed up in a single commandment, "You shall love your neighbor as yourself." If, however, you bite and devour one another, take care that you are not consumed by one another. Galatians 5:14-15*

# Patience

*This love of which I speak is slow to lose patience—*
*it looks for a way of being constructive.*
*1 Corinthians 13:4 (Phillips)*

You know how much I love the children, Lord, but I sure do lose patience with them sometimes. How do I look for ways of being constructive when I'm so tired and preoccupied? Lord, I need some of your creative power to be creative as a mother, to have imagination for new ways of coping.

Lord, I know patience often means waiting, but help me to wait kindly. You are patient with me; you wait for me to look to you in prayer. Help me to do that with the children. They require enormous patience these days. Help me not to yell, not to punish unfairly, not to expect too much. Give me constructive ways of dealing with them.

And help me to be patient with myself. Show me constructive ways of dealing with myself, healing ways that come from you. Let patience be a kind of peace, Lord.

*The farmer waits for the precious crop from the earth, being patient with it until it receives the early and the late rains.*
*James 5:7*

# Praise

*Parents, do not irritate your children, or they will become discouraged. Colossians 3:21 (GNB)*

*I will exalt you, my God the King; I will praise your name for ever and ever. Psalm 145:1 (NIV)*

O Lord, you seek our praise. The praise we give you seems more for our benefit than yours. When we praise, we think about all that you've done for us. Surely you do not need our praise, but we need to give it.

But you know, too, that we need praise. I don't get much at work these days. The people I work with are difficult, and that compounds this already difficult home situation. But I did get a "well done" on a paper I wrote for a class. That made my week!

Help me to give affirmation and praise to the children, Lord. There are so many things I have to correct them for or remind them about. I feel so alone in raising them; it makes me resentful. Then I grumble at them all the more. But could I find one thing to praise in them each day? And you call on us to praise your name. Can I use my children's names more in praise?

O Jesus, you called on your Father. You praised his name. Perhaps if I praise you more, the idea of praise will overflow and I can praise the children, maybe even someone at work.

O God, I praise you for graciously hearing my prayer, for meeting my needs through Jesus, my savior. I join with all creation to praise your name.

*Let everything that breathes praise the LORD! Psalm 150:6*

# Report Cards

*Each one should test his own actions. Then he can take pride in himself, without comparing himself to somebody else.*
*Galatians 6:4 (NIV)*

O God, I'm thankful you don't keep report cards on us. I would have flunked for sure. But you forgive, encourage, nurture, enable, restore your children.

The world isn't like that. There are grades to make in school and supervisor's evaluations to pass at work. The grades on the report cards can be helpful, but why do the children compare themselves so much with each other? It's as if the grade is the only thing, not what it tells about success in a subject or becoming more skilled.

Help me to instill in the children a sense of being proud of their own work, not having to compare themselves with someone else. Such freedom comes when we can forget what others are doing and work on our own goals. Do the children have goals? Do I? The counselor has talked with me about goals. Maybe we all need to talk about goals for our family and for us as individuals.

Maybe I can help them by talking about some of the goals in my own life. Lord, help me not to compare myself to others. Let my work speak for itself. Free me from harmful competition for its own sake. Free me to do well in my work for my own satisfaction and your glory.

*It is God who is at work in you, enabling you both to will and to work for his good pleasure. Philippians 2:13*

# Rules

*Parents, do not treat your children in such a way as to make them angry. Instead, raise them with Christian discipline and instruction. Ephesians 6:4 (GNB)*

This is a hard verse, Lord. The children *do* get angry with me, even when I think I'm being fair. We need rules in the household, but the children are always testing. When I was a teenager, I trained my dog. He learned the rules and that was that. Setting rules doesn't work with children. They know the rules, but they try to get around them.

Help me to be fair and consistent, Lord. Is it anger about unfair rules and inconsistent or harsh discipline that the Scripture speaks of here? I feel so wishy-washy at times. They wear me down when I'm tired. Help me, Lord, to be kind but firm. Help me not to feel guilty about enforcing rules.

"Dad lets us do anything we want," they say. "We don't have to go to bed this early at Dad's." I'm not sure that's true. And even if it is true, Lord, please help the children to understand and live by the rules we've made together for this household.

Lord, I know your commandments are for our good, but sometimes I look for ways around them. I, too, am like a child. But I trust your constant love and forgiveness. Help me to love and forgive the children and reiterate the rules, just as you do for me.

*The earth, O LORD, is full of your steadfast love; teach me your statutes. . . . Teach me good judgment and knowledge, for I believe in your commandments. Psalm 119:64,66*

# Runaway

*I have gone astray like a lost sheep; seek out your servant, for I do not forget your commandments. Psalm 119:176*

Four is certainly a stubborn age, Lord. He ran away in his pajamas this morning, down the street, past the neighbor's house, and I ran after him in my bathrobe. I thought of the picture of you, Lord, carrying a lost sheep on your shoulders. That's not the way it was with this screaming, kicking child. But somehow I kept my cool and didn't yell back. Somehow you helped me to show firm love that brought back the runaway. And he knew he was loved, that I wouldn't give up on him and let him run far. It wasn't long before we hugged.

Thank you, Lord, for calm in the midst of turmoil. As much as I want to live my life always aware of your loving presence, as much as I appreciate your good gifts, I still run away, too. Especially now, it seems. Divorce does odd things to people, at times making us run away even from friends and family who love us, and from you.

Sometimes you find me and draw me back in a joyful way, other times I seem to fight being found. Thank you for not giving up on me, Lord. Always come after me and bring me home when I stray. Thank you for such love.

*If I take the wings of the morning and settle at the farthest limits of the sea, even there your hand shall lead me, and your right hand shall hold me fast. Psalm 139:9-10*

# School

*Listen to advice and accept instruction, that you may gain wisdom for the future.* *Proverbs 19:20*

I loved school, Lord; my brother hated it. And now I have one child like me, one like my brother. These two daughters are so different. I end up spending a great deal of time with Tara and her studies and seeing the teacher about problems. Then I feel I'm neglecting my other daughter, who sails along smoothly in school.

Would things have been different for Tara if the divorce hadn't come? Intact families have kids with school troubles, too, but it seems worse for Tara now. Help me to help her, Lord. Give her understanding of her subjects. Give her some good times in school so her self-esteem will increase. Help me to show her how learning is beneficial.

Lord, bless the teachers at school. Help them in their enormous and difficult job.

*When you stop learning, you will soon neglect what you already know.* *Proverbs 19:27 (GNB)*

# Sergeant Mom

*Discipline your children, and they will give you rest; they will give delight to your heart. Proverbs 29:17*

Discipline—I think about it every day, Lord. I try to think of it as training, not punishment. But I have to be so tough, Lord. I feel like a sergeant. If I let down and relax the rules, the children run all over me. "Okay," I said, "you can watch one program tonight." But then they wanted another one, and pouted and said I was mean when I turned off the set after the one program.

I was trying to be nice, Lord, to let them have a little leeway on a school night. And it *was* a good program. Why couldn't they just appreciate watching it, and then go to bed? Why did the evening have to end up in an ugly scene again? I'm so tired of being Sergeant Mom.

Am I making too much of this evening? Do I feel worse than they do? Maybe. I guess I test you sometimes, Lord, and I want more when you've given so much already. I guess I hurt your feelings, yet you keep taking pleasure in your people, in me.

You can help me to keep all this in balance, Lord, and always to remember your love. Help me also to enjoy the children even when they need discipline, and not to weary of providing the discipline that is necessary.

*So let us not grow weary in doing what is right, for we will reap at harvest-time, if we do not give up. Galatians 6:9*

*Praise the LORD! Sing to the LORD a new song . . . for the LORD takes pleasure in his people. Psalm 149:1,4*

# Sickness

*When [Jesus] went ashore, he saw a great crowd; and he had compassion for them and cured their sick. Matthew 14:14*

Jesus, I'm glad there are so many references in the Bible to your caring for people who are sick. People are sick today, too, and you still care for them, healing them or giving them strength to endure their suffering.

Todd has been up half the night, not feeling well, and today I wonder what I ought to do. I guess I should take him to the doctor. But last time we went it was over nothing—but the bill wasn't "nothing"!

It's so hard handling sickness alone. I know I'm supposed to trust and not worry. But I worry about getting sick myself. And with Todd sick, I'm missing work again.

I feel so alone in this worry, Lord, and yet it seems every magazine for parents has an article about sickness—"Sickness and the Single Mom"; "When Mom Gets Sick"; "When to Take Your Child to the Doctor." I guess caring for sick children is a worry for lots of parents.

Help me to deal with it, Lord. Help guide our country as the government tries to deal with ongoing concerns about health problems and medical care for children, and sick leave for parents.

O Lord, I need your compassion and strength right now, today, and so does Todd.

*May you be made strong with all the strength that comes from his glorious power, and may you be prepared to endure everything with patience. Colossians 1:11*

# Solitude

*And after he had dismissed the crowds, he went up the mountain by himself to pray. When evening came, he was there alone. Matthew 14:23*

Today the children are with their grandparents and the house is quiet, but I am not lonely. Thank you, Lord. Sometimes I savor the quiet peacefulness when they are away. I feel alone and safe today, and that's a comforting surprise; my emotions have been so unpredictable lately.

I'm taking time this morning to read your Word. I read somewhere that Scripture is like a bridge, that it "vibrates" Christ to us, so we should read it even when we don't feel like it. But I'm glad to be quietly with you today, Lord.

Let your peace settle over me. Let it remain with me while I catch up on chores today. Make me aware of your presence in this solitude. Guide me in decisions I need to make today. Strengthen me for the busy, chaotic times that I know will come next week. You had busy times, Jesus. Were the moments of quiet solitude with your heavenly Father what helped you through the hectic times?

Tonight I'll have a bubble bath and a cup of tea. Let me think of these as blessings from you. I'm so used to feeling guilty about taking time for myself. Help me to feel your presence and know how necessary such times for relaxation and taking care of myself are.

*For thus said the Lord GOD, the Holy One of Israel: In returning and rest you shall be saved; in quietness and in trust shall be your strength. Isaiah 30:15*

# Talking/Listening/Looking

*When Jesus saw their faith, he said to the paralytic, "Take heart, son; your sins are forgiven."* *Matthew 9:2*

Jesus, you did not shut out the people who came to you, even in great crowds. You talked with them, you listened, you saw their needs. You related to people in a way that showed real caring about their personal lives.

I forget to listen to the children sometimes. I merely glance at one's finger painting while my mind is elsewhere. I halfway listen to another tell a story, but I don't always hear. It is hardest for me when they need to talk about the divorce. I know they need to get their feelings out, but I don't want to listen to their pain and anger. Help me to let them talk about their feelings, even though it hurts me. Help me to hear what's going on in their hearts and minds. Help me to see each child individually, to look at the one speaking, to really see and really hear. Lord, give me strength and peace and love enough to do that.

And help us to pray together about our mutual concerns, to pray for each other and with each other, coming to you together as people you love. We are all your children. I don't want to forget that I am your child, too.

*For [God] says, "At an acceptable time I have listened to you, and on a day of salvation I have helped you."*
*2 Corinthians 6:2*

# Time (never enough)

*For thus says the LORD, who created the heavens (he is God!), who formed the earth and made it (he established it; he did not create it a chaos, he formed it to be inhabited!).*
*Isaiah 45:18*

O Lord, you created order and beauty. You created time, so that we could have order in our lives, not chaos. And yet it seems as if there's never enough time. Time seems to run out and chaos results. Again and again I get myself organized, and then it all slips out of whack. I find myself rushing again, with anxiety as my companion.

I come to you at this time, Lord. Teach me, show me. I must seek you in your Word, even if the time to do so will be brief. Don't let me put this aside. Even three minutes with your Word is healthier than none.

Why must I learn again and again not to neglect spending time with you, Lord? When I have even a few moments with you each day, order comes to my life, my days seem less chaotic. But then I miss a day or two, and I'm rushing again and not finding time for you. Help me again, Lord, for myself and for the children. Help me to organize my time again, starting with time spent with you.

*Sow for yourselves righteousness; reap steadfast love; break up your fallow ground; for it is time to seek the LORD, that he may come and rain righteousness upon you.* *Hosea 10:12*

# Tired

*The LORD is the everlasting God, the Creator of the ends of the earth. He does not faint or grow weary. Isaiah 40:28*

I am so tired, Lord. All the time. Maybe some of it is depression. I don't sleep well at night, so I wake up tired on so many mornings. It's a heavy kind of tired that I feel, a weariness that is always just below the surface. It helps to talk about it, Lord, to pray and tell you how I feel.

I think of women in the Bible I learned about in Sunday school. They had tired, depressed times too. Sarah and Hannah waiting to get pregnant, Ruth being a widow and helping her mother-in-law. And didn't your mother, Mary, feel exhausted after your crucifixion? All the women who come to mind suffered from tiredness and probably knew what it feels like to be depressed. The Samaritan woman at the well. The woman with the hemorrhage for twelve years. But she touched your clothes and was made well.

Touch me, Lord. Hold me and help me to know that you are working in my life right now. I feel empty and in need of the strength you give.

*He gives power to the faint, and strengthens the powerless. Even youths will faint and be weary . . . but those who wait for the LORD shall renew their strength, they shall mount up with wings like eagles, they shall run and not be weary, they shall walk and not faint. Isaiah 40:29-31*

# Touch

*Simon's mother-in-law was sick in bed with a fever, . . .*
*[Jesus] went to her, took her by the hand, and helped her up.*
*The fever left her, and she began to wait on them.*
*Mark 1:30-31 (GNB)*

O God, I never realized a hug could feel so good. She's just an acquaintance at church, but somehow she sensed my loneliness today and gave me a hug after we exchanged a few words about the weather. I felt a wholeness in that hug; I was affirmed as a person and as part of the family of your church.

Touching—it seems so important now that I'm alone. A handshake, a pat on the arm, a hug. You came in the flesh, Jesus; you understand our physical nature. You know that we were created to need each other in physical ways.

Help me to realize my child's needs, too. Sometimes I'm so caught up inside myself that I forget. On Friday I was late for work and rushed out without giving Kate the usual goodbye hug. No wonder she was distant that evening. I remember when she was little and would come to where I was working in the house and stand there just to be near. She still does, at times. Give me patience to stop what I'm doing and give attention—a touch or a hug.

Jesus, you often touched people when you healed them. It was faith that made them well, but they could be very sure of your caring because of your touch. Help me to be like that.

In Holy Communion you still touch me and I touch you. Thank you for such love.

*. . . [Jesus] said, "This is my body that is for you ."*
*1 Corinthians 11:24*

# TV

*Whatever is true, whatever is noble, whatever is right, whatever is pure, whatever is lovely, whatever is admirable—if anything is excellent or praiseworthy—think about such things. Philippians 4:8 (NIV)*

Thank you, God. I needed to hear that verse today—fill your minds with those things that are true, noble, lovely. Some of what is on TV these days may be true but it's not often admirable or pure or lovely. The kids understood my reasons when I talked to them about limiting how much they watch TV.

Lord, you know we've been through this before. I say no TV except selected programs on weekends. Then something comes up during the week or I'm depressed and can't be firm. I relent. Television is such an instrument for good or evil.

"Does that mean videos, too?" they ask. The kids can wear me down. I guess people tried to wear you down, Jesus, questioning your authority, looking for ways around what you said.

But I read this passage from Philippians to the children, and it seemed to make sense to them. For once we had a good discussion about TV and videos. Help us to stick with our new decision for regulating TV watching. Help us to find more creative uses of our time so we will think pure and worthwhile thoughts.

*The fruit of the Spirit is love, joy, peace, patience, kindness, generosity, faithfulness, gentleness, and self-control. There is no law against such things. Galatians 5:22-23*

# Vacations

*Then he [Elijah] lay down under the broom tree and fell asleep. Suddenly an angel touched him and said to him, "Get up and eat." He looked, and there at his head was a cake baked on hot stones, and a jar of water. He ate and drank, and lay down again. The angel of the LORD came a second time, touched him, and said, "Get up and eat, otherwise the journey will be too much for you."  1 Kings 19:5-7*

Lord, everyone at work is talking about vacations, where they're going, what they're going to do. Others come in with pictures of where they've been. I feel so left out.

How can I afford to take a vacation? There's no money for it—or time for it. But I need *something*, some sort of time out. Lord, help me find a way to stop running at this mad pace.

Your angels ministered to Elijah and wouldn't let him go on without rest and refreshment. You gave us the sabbath—a time of rest. You made us, you know us, you call us to rest awhile. Will you provide the way, the insight for how I can find rest in my circumstances? Even a day or two of something different—that would be a vacation—a time of refreshment—a sabbath.

Give me creative thoughts on how to work this out. Help me to break out of this grind and be re-created for what's ahead.

*So then, a sabbath rest still remains for the people of God; for those who enter God's rest also cease from their labors as God did from his.  Hebrews 4:9-10*

# Weather

*"Have you entered the storehouses of the snow or seen the storehouses of the hail . . .? What is the way to the place where the lightning is dispersed. . . ? Does the rain have a father? Who fathers the drops of dew? From whose womb comes the ice?*
*Job 38:22,24a, 28-29a (NIV)*

O Jesus, you stilled the storm, you quieted the winds. You showed God's power over forces of weather. Help me to cope with difficult weather. These days my moods are affected so easily by the weather, more so than I ever remember in the past. A sunny day often means a sunny me. A stormy day means a stormy me. Jesus, you seemed to have patience and peace no matter what the weather. Help me. Give me peace, O Lord.

The children enjoy the weather changes. They love the snow, they want to play in the rain, they make up games about the thunder and lightning. Why do I think the only good weather is a temperate, sunny day?

Give me a creative spirit, Lord, to deal with weather in a new way. Keep my soul from fretting. Sometimes in your Word you are called the Sun. Be the sun in my life on dark, damp days. Call me into your Word, where I will find you. Open my eyes to the beauty of your world on any day. Let me marvel at the creative forces in any kind of weather. And let me be prepared and patient.

*The LORD has been mindful of us; he will bless us.*
*Psalm 115:12*

# What If I Die?

*Jesus said to her, "I am the resurrection and the life. Those who believe in me, even though they die, will live."*
*John 11:25*

Lord, the question comes and I try to push it back, but it will not be silent. What if I die? What if I die tomorrow? I am cold thinking of it. What would happen to Jenny?

Her father would raise her, maybe. Or my sister. Or the grandparents. We haven't worked it out on paper yet. Lord, does the question keep coming to prod me into doing the hard legal things? The will. The insurance.

I trust you with my future, living or dying, because of Jesus' resurrection. And I know you love Jenny, that somehow life will be okay for her, even if I die while she's growing up. My cousin's mother died when he was four. It was awful and confusing for him for a while. Later he learned to love his stepmother, but the family kept alive the memory of his mother with stories and pictures. He's grown now but he loves his mother. There is a relationship between them, even though she died long ago.

Lord, give me the resolve and understanding to do what's needed legally for Jenny's protection. Then give me peace that, living or dying, I am with you and so is Jenny.

*I will pour my spirit upon your descendants, and my blessing on your offspring. . . . Do not fear, or be afraid; . . . There is no other rock; I know not one. Isaiah 44:3,8*

# Wishful Thinking

*The wolf shall live with the lamb, the leopard shall lie down with the kid. Isaiah 11:6*

"When Daddy comes back home to live"—I overheard Jake saying this to one of his little friends. Lord, Jake's always indulging in wishful thinking. I've read that this kind of wishful thinking is common for kids of divorce. They keep imagining the parents back together. And yet I know I need to help Jake accept reality—that Daddy isn't coming back home to live, that Jake has two parents who love him, but they live at different addresses.

I heard a sermon once about the Isaiah verse that speaks of the future time when the wolf shall live with the lamb. But, the pastor said, the wolf will still be a wolf and the lamb will still be a lamb. The wolf won't eat up the lamb, though, and the lamb won't be scared.

Lord, I hope Jake's dad and I can get along well enough to be at family functions, like graduations and weddings, in a peaceful sort of way. Help me to explain to Jake that this is the most he can expect of us. The wolf will still be a wolf and the lamb will still be a lamb, but we'll try to get along well enough to both be at the same family functions, for Jake's sake. Help us all to be content with that much peacefulness, after all that has happened.

*There is great gain in godliness combined with contentment. 1 Timothy 6:6*

# Work

*Commit your work to the LORD, and your plans will be established. Proverbs 16:3*

Work really gets to me sometimes, Lord. I'm lucky to be in a career field I chose, but the pressures of job and children and home are overwhelming these days. I never thought it would be like this. I'd imagined being able to work part-time when the children were small. I guess I figured on "having it all," as the expression goes. But this "all" now is too much, Lord.

There are personality issues to deal with at work, reports to complete, standards to be met. I enjoy the work, but I'm worn out when I get home. But I can't be worn out—I have to be a mommy and a homemaker. Then come memories of growing up with my mom at home. Often there were fresh baked cookies after school. I talked, she listened, relaxed and smiling. She worked part-time at something she loved, but could always be there for us, too.

I need to work full-time now, but memories of my own childhood haunt me and I want that kind of life for my children. It's very confusing, Lord. My mother told me of *her* childhood, when her mother taught school full-time. She remembers being in all-day nursery school, as they called it. Her memories are happy. Lord, help me to accept the way life is now; guide me in my work and schedule and give me energy.

*For we are what he has made us, created in Christ Jesus for good works, which God prepared beforehand to be our way of life. Ephesians 2:10*

# Worry

*"So do not worry about tomorrow; it will have enough worries of its own. There is no need to add to the troubles each day brings."  Matthew 6:34 (GNB)*

Worry grabs me by the throat and feels like panic sometimes, Lord. When I was a little kid at the ocean, a big wave knocked me down and swept over me. I couldn't breathe. I thought I'd never get up. Worry does that to me, Lord. It knocks me down; it tries to strangle me. The children are always on my mind, the bills, the constant stress of all the things that have to be done, big and little. The "what if?" trap catches me. Even my prayers are lists of worries. Help me, O Lord.

Help me to focus on other things, Lord. Thank you for the Scriptures that tell me you care. Thank you for people who tell me they care. I see all this caring in little ways and big ways, when I stop a moment to think and remember. Maybe I'll make a list of things to thank you for. I guess that's what some of the psalmists did. They started out with lots of worries and complaints and ended with thanks for past blessings. But I can only do this with your help, Lord. Please help today.

*Do not fear, for I am with you, do not be afraid, for I am your God; I will strengthen you, I will help you, I will uphold you with my victorious right hand.  Isaiah 41:10*

# Worship

*I pray to you, O LORD; you hear my voice in the morning; at sunrise I offer my prayer and wait for your answer. . . . Because of your great love I can come into your house; I can worship in your holy Temple and bow down to you in reverence. Psalm 5:2-3,7 (GNB)*

"Life is too short to wait to become faithful," I read in my devotional booklet this morning, Lord. That quotation got me up and out with the children to church this morning. I want to be there most Sundays, but sometimes I'm tired. Sometimes everything seems different. But I know that although I talk to you, Lord, throughout the day, I also need to be in church, worshiping with others Christians on Sunday. Their faith buoys up my faith. Their frustration with their own rambunctious children lets me know I'm not alone with mine.

I know, Jesus, that I go because you made it possible for me to stand before God. Your love makes worship possible for me, for us. And at worship, I'm a child, too, coming to a loving parent for nurture and forgiveness and love. Thank you for welcoming me today.

*Come to me, all you that are weary and are carrying heavy burdens, and I will give you rest. Take my yoke upon you, and learn from me; for I am gentle and humble in heart, and you will find rest for your souls. Matthew 11:28-29*

# Your Will/My Will/Their Will

*You are my God; teach me to do your will. Be good to me, and guide me on a safe path. Psalm 143:10 (GNB)*

*Correction and discipline are good for children. If a child has his own way, he will make his mother ashamed of him. Proverbs 29:15 (GNB)*

Lord, so often I think of "will" as "want." What I want, what the kids want, what you want. And so often none of these wants seems to agree. My daughter wants to be on the school field hockey team, despite slipping grades. I want her to get her grades up before we talk about sports.

Lord, what do you want in all this? What is your will? For her to honor her parent? For me to raise her well, to know and to love and to serve you and others? How does *your* will fit with the problem of *my* will and *her* will? It seems such a stalemate. And am I afraid to look at your will, because of the divorce?

*Your will*—now I remember. It's not just what you want us to do, it's what you want to do for us. You want to love us, to share your peace and strength and forgiveness with us. You are the main "doer" here. You do *your* will for us, for me, for the children. Thank you, Lord.

How can I do my will for my daughter? How can I love her? Is it by helping her with the math so her grades won't fall and she *can* be on the team? Lord, help me to love her that much.

*This, then, is how you should pray: "Our Father in heaven: May your holy name be honored; may your Kingdom come; may your will be done on earth as it is in heaven." Matthew 6:9-10 (GNB)*